How to Simply Cut Hair Even Better

An advanced step by step guide to the
six basic haircuts that can be combined or
altered to create just about any hairstyle.

Written and illustrated by

Laurie Punches

Published by Punches Productions
South Lake Tahoe, California

Punches, Laurie C.
How to Simply Cut Hair Even Better
"A Punches Productions Book."

Publisher's cataloging in Publication Data
1. Haircutting (advanced). I. Punches, Laurie.
1.Title

1 2 3 4 5 6 7 8 9 10

Library of Congress Catalog Number
88-92468

ISBN 0-929833-08-X

To make haircutting an easier and more enjoyable experience... **we have made the following teaching aids available to you.** Just fill out and send in the order form located in the back of this book. For prompt delivery dial 1-(800)/833-8778 to order.

A HAIRCUTTING KIT $29.95
Professional 5" ice-tempered haircutting scissors, a plastic haircutting cape, a 7" plastic all-purpose comb marked in inches, a neck duster brush, a spray bottle and five plastic butterfly clamps packed in a nylon duffle bag for convenient storage.

HOW TO SIMPLY... VIDEOS
"How to Simply Cut Hair"	$29.95
"How to Simply Cut Children's Hair"	$29.95
"How to Simply Perm Hair"	$19.95
"How to Simply Highlight Hair"	$19.95

These instructional videos follow the same step by step instructions found in the books.

HOW TO SIMPLY.... BOOKS
"How to Simply Cut Hair" (beginners haircutting)	$10.95
"How to Simply Cut Hair Even Better" (advanced haircutting)	$12.95
"How to Simply Cut Children's Hair"	$7.95
"How to Simply Perm Hair"	$6.95
"How to Simply Highlight Hair"	$6.95

A PRACTICE DOLL HEAD $24.95
This manikin head and holder has 19" long human hair. It attaches to just about any table, desk or counter top providing hours of haircutting practice... **at your own pace!**

ACKNOWLEDGEMENTS

The author would like to acknowledge the help and support of Jack Rogers and Mark Rayburn for layout, design and production, Debbie Rogers, Rod Ruple and Carla Martinez for editing, Steve Björkman for the cover illustration, Virgil Masalta for the author's photograph and my huband Peter, for the hours spent caring for our children during the many hours devoted to writing and illustrating this book. Thank you very much.

DEDICATION

This book is dedicated to Peter, Ryan, Katie, Michael and Jeffrey, my lovable troop.

DISCLAIMER

This book in no way claims to be a substitute for beauty school. It is merely a haircutting guide for the non-professional to be used in the home. The word "client" simply refers to the person who's hair is being cut. No professionalism is inferred.

TABLE OF CONTENTS

FOREWORD

This book is an advanced haircutting guide that is intended to follow the book, "How to Simply Cut Hair", written for beginners. It teaches more advanced methods to the six basic haircuts and how they can be combined and altered to create just about any hairstyle.

Even if you have very little knowledge or experience cutting hair, this book can teach you how to cut anyone's hair. This step by step guide to haircutting can be used for all types of hair whether long, short, thick, fine, straight, or curly. Haircutting for men and women is identical, the only variables being length and angles. Fashions and styles will keep on changing, but basic haircutting always stays the same.

An instructional video that teaches the six basic haircuts, along with other teaching aids such as: **a haircutting kit, practice doll head** and **other instructional books on haircutting, perming, and highlighting hai**r can be ordered by filling out and sending the attached card at the back of this book.

INTRODUCTION

This book teaches the six basic haircuts and how they can be combined and altered to create just about any hairstyle imaginable.

There are three ingredients needed to be successful at cutting hair.

The first ingredient is to have a strong **desire to learn**. This desire may be to save money by stretching the time between professional haircuts, or to cut your family and friend's hair.

The second ingredient needed is the **knowledge of haircutting** which this book will provide.

The third ingredient is the **willingness to try** each of the six basic haircuts taught in this book.

Soon you will become familiar with each of the six basic haircuts and be combining and altering them to create various hairstyles. For example the same haircut can be changed by parting the hair on either side or down the middle. It can be combed forward, pulled back off the face, sculpted, gelled, blow dried or left natural. Sideburns can be left long, medium, short, angled, straight, or softly slanted. Perming and highlighting can give hair the personality and texture needed for achieving the look you want.

Before starting the haircutting process you will need to take a rcalistic look at the person's hair you are about to cut. This person will be addressed as the "client" throughout the remainder of this book. The client will be referred to in the feminine gender throughout this book with the exception of the section on shorter haircuts where the masculine gender will be used.

COMMUNICATION

Take the time to discuss what hairstyle your client wants. The most common complaint is, "she didn't cut my hair the way I wanted it cut". Communication is the key to successful haircutting. Take the time to listen to what your client wants in her hairstyle. Repeat what you heard her say. Listen to and repeat what your client said until you have a crystal clear picture of the desired hairstyle. Some helpful questsions to ask might be: How much length do you want taken off? Do you want a part? If so, where? Do you want bangs? If so, how much and how long? Do you want a sharp blunt line or a soft wispy look to your cut? How much ear would you like exposed?

In helping your client choose her hairstyle, you want to choose a cut that will give her face the appearance of being perfectly oval. Longer layers can give the illusion of having thick, full hair which can make the narrower face appear wider. Height can be added by cutting shorter layers at the crown. Never draw attention to the areas of width by having the finished length end at the point of greatest width. This will only emphasize the width that you are trying to camouflauge. You want to draw attention to other areas. Long bangs can also take away length from the face, adding the illusion of width.

HAIR TEXTURE

There are many textures and types of hair: thick, medium, thin, curly, wavy, straight, coarse, medium and fine. Most hair can be cut by simply following the directions in this book. Here are a few helpful suggestions for problems you might encounter.

Straight, Fine Hair

When you cut straight, fine hair, unwanted, choppy cutting lines are often left in the hair. Tiny, steep, triangle shaped slivers can be cut into the very ends of your client's hair to break up these harsh lines. This technique is taught later in the chapter "Alterations".

Curly Hair

Curly hair has the tendency to shrink when it is dry. The tighter the curl, the more shrinkage will result once the hair is dry. To compensate for this loss in length, leave the hair a little bit longer than you think is needed.

12

Thick Hair

Sometimes when you are cutting thick or coarse hair, you will find your scissors unable to easily cut through the thickness. If this is the case, take a smaller amount of hair down with each parting in a section, instead of trying to cut it all at once.

Wavy Hair

Wavy hair is the easiest and the most forgiving hair to cut. The soft, natural curvature will hide most slight imperfections.

The purpose of this book is to teach the art of haircutting, not to just memorize haircuts. If you combine the knowledge you learn from this book with experience and your own creativity, you will soon be able to cut just about anyone's hair with confidence.

1

THE SHOP SET-UP

Don't spend too much time and energy worrying about where to set up shop. Just about any place will do. I've even cut hair with my client sitting on top of a trash can in a campground during a rainstorm!

The bathroom seems to lend itself well to haircutting. A large mirror, good lighting, an easy to clean floor, and a convenient counter top where tools can easily be reached makes haircutting an easier and much more enjoyable experience

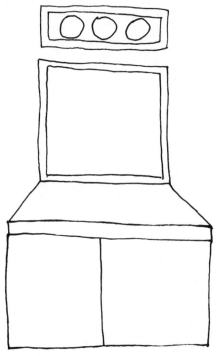

2

THE TOOLS

In order to cut hair well, you will need a small assortment of tools. This ensemble consists of a pair of ice-tempered, stainless steel, professional haircutting scissors, a plastic all-purpose comb marked in inches, a waterproof cape, a spray bottle, a neck duster and five plastic butterfly hair clips. **You can order an inexpensive, quality kit that contains these tools by filling out and sending the form located in the back of this book**. These tools may also be purchased individually at your local beauty or barber supply. A small investment in quality tools will make haircutting a much more enjoyable learning experience.

SCISSORS

A pair of 5" ice-tempered, stainless steel professional haircutting scissors with a finger tang. This is the most important tool for precision haircutting.

COMB

A 7" plastic, all-purpose comb marked in inches for measuring and comparing hair lengths throughout the haircut.

CAPE

A large piece of waterproof or water resistant material that fastens at the back of the neck to protect your client from pieces of cut hair.

SPRAY BOTTLE

An 8 ounce plastic mister or spritzer. This spray bottle is used to keep your client's hair wet throughout the haircut.

NECK DUSTER

This brush can be used quickly and easily to remove pieces of cut hair that tend to cling to your client's face, neck and clothes. It will lessen the possiblility of itching and discomfort that can be caused by these hairs.

BUTTERFLY CLAMPS

Five 2" butterfly clamps or five long, thin metal hair clips can assist you by keeping unwanted hair up and out of the way while cutting.

(EXTRA TOOLS)

APRON

A piece of waterproof or water resistant material that fastens around the stylist's neck and waist. It is used to protect the stylist from pieces of cut hair as well as chemicals such as perm solution, bleach, peroxide and tint.

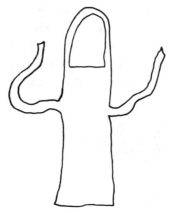

ELECTRIC RAZOR

This is the least necessary and most expensive tool in haircutting. Most haircutting kits are built around the razor rather than the scissors which focuses on cutting hair for men and boys. The "Short Layered Cut" taught in this book is similar to a razor cut given at a barber shop. A razor can also be used to remove excess neck, sideburn and moustache hair. If you don't already have access to a razor, there is an alternative method using scissors taught in the chapter, "Alterations".

THINNING SHEARS

Thinning shears are used to take out unwanted bulk and thickness in your client's hair. They look like scissors with teeth on either one or both blades. An alternative method of thinning hair using scissors is also taught in the chapter, "Alterations".

BLOWDRYER AND CURLING IRON

A blowdryer and curling iron are the tools most often used to style and complete your finished haircuts.

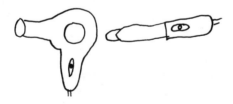

These are the tools used for cutting and styling hair... and this is a picture of a typical shop set-up.

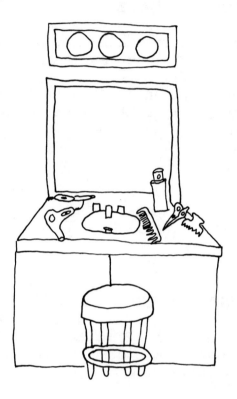

3

TO START

BRUSHING

Start your cut by thoroughly brushing the hair. This will loosen any dry scalp flakes and bring the natural oils from the scalp to the hair ends. The bristles will help to massage the scalp and stimulate good blood circulation as well as eliminate snarls.

SHAMPOO

After a good brushing, always start with a freshly washed head of hair. This will make the hair more manageable and pliable. Apply a small amount of shampoo, massage well and rinse until the hair is free of suds. Repeat this step if necessary. Now rinse the hair one last time using cold water. The cold water will help remove any lingering trace of shampoo that often leaves a dull film or residue in the hair

CONDITION

A conditioner may be applied if your client's hair is dry or full of tangles. Squeeze a moderate amount of conditioner into the palm of your hand, rub your hands together and distribute the conditioner evenly to the ends of the hair. Work it through the rest of the hairshafts. Now rinse the hair with tepid water...

Rinse one last time with cold water to give the hair extra shine and towel dry.

4

HANDYWORK

Learning to hold and manipulate the scissors and comb will come with practice. At first it may seem awkward, but don't get discouraged. Soon it will be second nature. Be sure to take the time needed to read and practice this "handywork" until it feels comfortable before going any further.

HOLDING THE SCISSORS

Begin by placing the thumb of your most dexterous hand through the large hole and your ring finger through the small hole of the scissors. Rest your pinky on the finger tang. The scissors will stay in this hand while the comb will continually change hands.

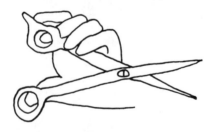

HOLDING THE COMB

Slip just your thumb out of the large scissor hole and lay the scissors in the palm of your most dexterous hand. Place the comb in the same hand between the index finger and thumb. Now comb the hair using the wide tooth end of the comb.

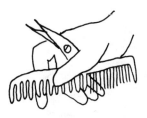

With your free hand, grasp your client's hair between your index and middle fingers. Slide your fingers down the hair shaft applying just enough pressure to create tension. Your fingers should stop sliding just above the point at which the hair will be cut.

COMB EXCHANGE

While still holding the hair between the index and middle fingers of your less dexterous hand, place the comb in the same hand, between the thumb and index finger.

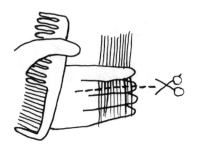

CUTTING

Place the thumb of your more dexterous hand back through the large hole of the scissors. Cut the hair just beneath the index and middle fingers holding the hair. Use these fingers as a straight edge and cut parallel to them.

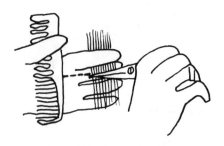

5

BANGS

There are four types of bangs: fringe, light, medium and heavy, ranging from sheer bangs to full bangs.

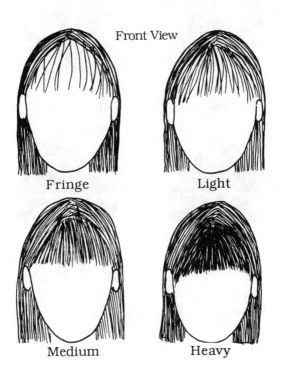

Front View

Fringe   Light

Medium   Heavy

To create bangs you will be using a semicircle part which will extend from one temple to the other. A more shallow semicircle creates fewer bangs, while a deeper semicircle creates fuller bangs. Decide from the following pictures how much bangs are desired.

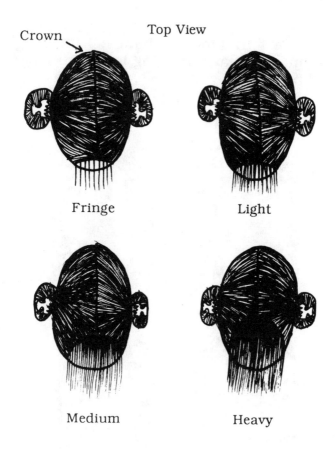

Top View

Crown

Fringe

Light

Medium

Heavy

Now part the hair in a semicircle leaving a fringe, light, medium or heavy bang section. Comb the remaining hair away from your client's face and clip it up and out of the way.

This will help define the bang section.

Fringe　　　　Light

Medium　　　Heavy

Comb the bang section forward. Make a semicircle part from temple to temple bringing
down just a fringe of hair from the hairline.
Clip the rest of the bang section up in another clip. Comb the sheer bang parting forward
laying the wet fringe hair flat against your
client's forehead.

Decide upon the length and the contour of the bangs. Do you want a soft curved line or a straight blunt line?

Use the distance between the bridge and the tip of your client's nose as a measuring tape.

Short –
Medium –
Long –

Cutting the hair closer to the bridge creates a shorter bang while cutting closer to the tip creates a longer bang length.

Comb the bang fringe flat against your client's forehead with the wide tooth end of the comb.

Cut these bangs to the desired length and contour.   Keep in mind that wet hair will shrink in length when it is dry.

If a shallow semicircle for fringe bangs was chosen, **the fringe bang is now finished.**

Make another one-third inch, semicircle part above the last parting. Comb the new parting of bangs down over the cut bangs with the wide tooth end of the comb. Clip the rest of the bang section back up and out of the way.

Decide whether you want all one length or layered bangs. If no layers are desired, comb the new bang parting flat over the just cut bangs. You should be able to see the cut bangs through the uncut bang parting. Using the cut bangs as a guide, cut the new parting of hair to the same length and contour. Begin at your client's left temple move toward the center and end at her right temple.

Layers are a result of the hair being elevated while being cut. This causes the ends to have less weight which creates a softer, fuller look.

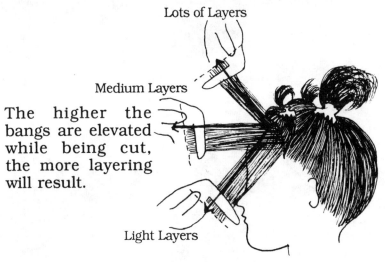

Lots of Layers

Medium Layers

The higher the bangs are elevated while being cut, the more layering will result.

Light Layers

If layers are desired, look at the following

pictures and determine how much layering is wanted.

Light Layers

Medium Layers

Lots of Layers

Hold both the cut bangs and the one-third inch parting of uncut bangs between the index and middle fingers of your less dexterous hand. Using the previous pictures, pull these bang hairs to the chosen elevation. You should be able to see the just cut bangs beneath the uncut bang parting.

Cut the new bang parting to the same length and contour as the just cut bangs at the chosen elevation.

If a semicircle for light bangs was chosen, **the light bang is now finished**.

Make another semicircle part one-third inch above the last parting. Comb the new bang parting down over the cut bangs with the wide tooth end of the comb. Clip the rest of the bang section back up and out of the way.

If no layering is wanted, comb the new bang parting flat over the cut bangs.

Using the cut bangs as a guide, cut the new bang parting to the same length and contour. Begin at your client's left temple move toward the center and end at her right temple.

If layers are desired, hold both the cut bangs and the one-third inch uncut bang parting between the index and middle fingers of your less dexterous hand.

Pull the hair to the same elevation used to cut the last bang parting. Using the cut bangs beneath as a guide, cut the new bang parting to the same length and contour.

If a semicircle for medium bangs was chosen, **the medium bang is now finished.**

Comb the remaining bang hairs down over the rest of the cut bangs using the wide tooth end of the comb.

If no layers are wanted, comb the entire bang section flat against your client's forehead. Using the cut bangs beneath as a guide, cut the remaining bang hairs to the same length and contour. Begin at your client's left temple move toward the center and end at her right temple.

If layers are desired, hold the entire bang section between the index and middle fingers of your less dexterous hand.

Pull the bang section to the same elevation chosen throughout this chapter. Using the cut bangs beneath as a guide, cut the remaining bang hairs to the same length and contour.

The heavy bang is now finished.

Now that the bangs have been cut, you may begin the haircut of your choice.

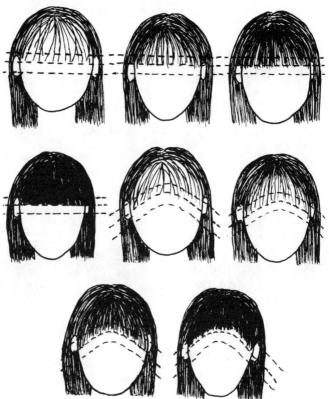

6

CUT 1

THE 'ALL ONE LENGTH' OR BLUNT CUT

The first cut is called the 'all one length' cut because all of the hair is cut to exactly the same length. This creates a blunt edge.

Follow the directions for: The Shop Set-up, The Tools, To Start, Handywork and Bangs before beginning this haircut.

Have your client part her own hair where she desires. If no part is wanted, part her hair down the middle to create symmetry.

Using a "T" part, divide your client's hair into four equal sections. This is done by drawing one part from ear to ear and the other part from the center forehead to center nape.

The parts should cross at the crown.

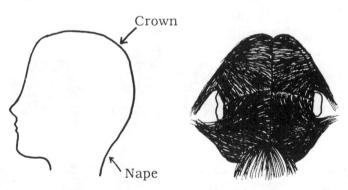

Clip each of these four sections up and out of the way.

Now make a part (approximately one-third inch from the hairline) around the entire head. Clip the rest of the hair back up into the four sections. This will create a fringe of hair around the perimeter or outline of your client's head.

Comb the fringe of hair straight down using the wide tooth end of the comb.

Cut a few strands in the very front of your client's right side to the desired length. Keep in mind wet hair will shrink when it is dry.

Now do the same with a few strands from the very front of your client's left side so that the cut lengths on both sides match.

46

Check to be sure that both sides are even by standing directly in front of your client at eye level. Take a pinch of hair from both sides and pull them tautly. Are both sides the same length?

If both sides are not even, cut off just a little length at a time from the longer side until the two sides are even and at the desired length.

Now you want to connect both cut side lengths by cutting the back.

Start by using the cut hair on your client's right side as a guide to match the hair laying beside it in length. Using your, 'handywork', comb the hair on your client's right side straight down. Cut the hair laying beside the already cut hair to the indentical length.

Now move slightly to your client's left.

Repeat the last step moving slowly from your client's right side toward the back and ending on her left side.

When you meet the pre-cut strands of hair on her left side all the fringe hairs outlining the head should now be cut to the same length.

This fringe will serve as a guide for length throughout the rest of this haircut.

49

Make another part (about 1" from the last part) around the entire head. Clip the rest of the hair back up into the four sections.

Comb this hair straight down over the cut fringe using the wide tooth end of the comb.

Begin on your client's right side. You should be able to see the cut fringe length beneath the new section of uncut hair. If not take down a little less hair so that you can see the cut lengths through the new parting. Using your handywork, cut the new parting of hair to the identical length as the fringe underneath. Start on your client's right side, slowly move toward the back, and end on her left side. This new parting should now be completely cut.

Make another part (approximately 2" from the last part) around your client's head. Clip the rest of the hair back up into the four sections.

Comb this new parting of hair over the cut

hairs with the wide tooth end of the comb.

Using the cut length beneath as a guide for length cut the new parting of hair to the identical length. Work from your client's right toward her back and end on her left. This parting should now be completely cut.

Take another parting (approximately 2")

around your client's head. Clip the rest of the hair back up into the four sections.

Work from your client's right, toward the back, ending on her left, cutting this parting of hair to the same length as the cut hair beneath.

Repeat the last two steps:1) Take down 2" partings. 2) Cut the new parting to the same length as the cut hair beneath (starting on your client's right, moving toward the center, and ending on her left). Do this until the en-

tire head of hair has been cut to the same
length.

Check once more to be sure that both sides
are even by standing directly in front of your
client at eye level. Take a pinch of hair from
both sides and pull them tautly. Are both
sides even?

If both sides are not even, cut off just a little length at a time from the longer side until the two sides are even and at the desired length.

If the length on either side or back needs adjusting, cut any longer hairs. to create a consistent and even length.

Comb the hair straight down using the **wide tooth end** of the comb. Cut any uneven hairs along the bottom edge to create a clean line.

Keeping your client's head held erect and

facing straight foreward, comb her hair one last time using the **fine tooth end** of the comb. Cut any stray hairs you might have missed along the bottom.

Now you have completed the 'all one length' cut and the hair is ready to be styled.

7

CUT 2

THE "UNDER CUT"

This haircut is also referred to as 'the bob' or 'pageboy'. The undercut requires the underneath hairs to be cut to a shorter length than the top or surface hairs. This graduation from shorter to longer lengths causes the ends to softly curve under. This particular haircut will require some cooperation from your client who must respond to your gently pushing her head and neck in various positions.

Follow the directions for: The Shop Set-up, The Tools, To Start, Handywork, and Bangs before beginning this haircut.

Have your client part her own hair where she desires. If no part is wanted, part her hair down the middle to create symmetry.

Using a "T" parting, divide the hair into four equal sections. This is done by drawing one part from ear to ear and the other from mid-forehead to center nape.

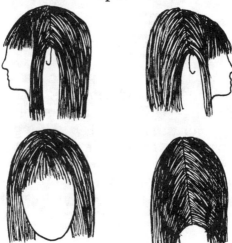

The parts should cross at the crown.

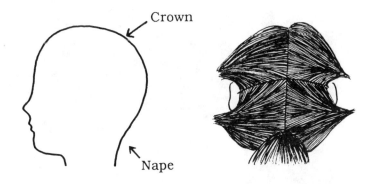

Clip each of the four sections up into seperate clips.

Now make a part (approximately one-third inch from the hairline) around the entire head. Clip the rest of the hair back up into the four sections. This will create a fringe of hair around the perimeter or outline of your client's head.

Comb the fringe hairs straight down using the wide tooth end of the comb.

Looking at the following pictures, **choose one that most closely defines the outline of your client's desired haircut.** (Outline 7 has been selected in the pictures throughout this chapter.)

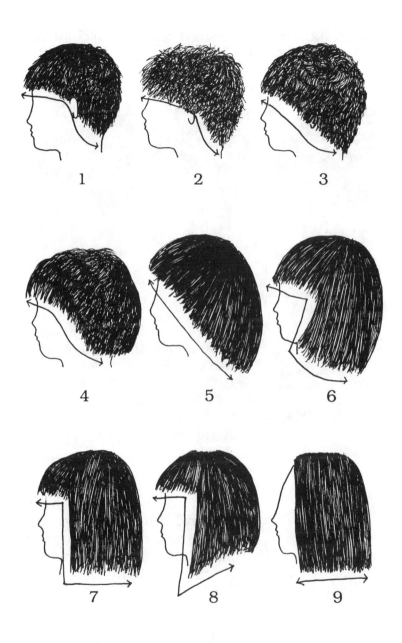

1   2   3

4   5   6

7   8   9

Beginning on your client's right, cut the

fringe hair to the desired lengths needed for your chosen outline.

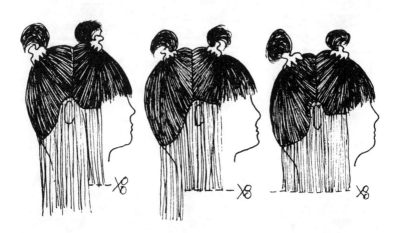

When **cutting hair over the ears**, take care not to nip them. Press the ear flat against your client's head with your less dexterous hand while cutting.

If you are **cutting hair around the ears**, press each ear forward with your less dexterous hand while cutting the hair.

After cutting the fringe on your client's right side to the necessary lengths to create your chosen outline, do the same to the back...

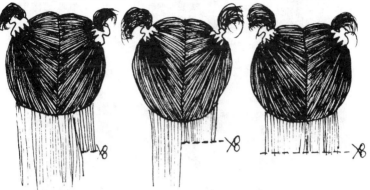

left side...

and front of your client's head.

The fringe outlining your client's head should now be finished. It will serve as a guide for length throughout the rest of this haircut.

Make another part (approximately 1" from the last part) around the entire head. Clip the rest of the hair back up into the four sections.

Comb this hair down over the cut hairs using the wide tooth end of the comb.

Stand on your client's right side. Press your client's head all the way to her left side until her left ear is resting on her shoulder. Comb and press the wet hair flat against the right side of your client's face and neck so that it sticks to the skin. Now cut the surface hairs to the same length as the cut hairs underneath.

Stand in back of your client. Push her head completely forward until her chin rests on her collar bone. Comb your client's hair with the wide tooth end of the comb laying the wet hair flat against the back of her head and bent neck so that it sticks to the skin. Cut your client's hair in the back to the same length as the cut hair beneath.

Stand on your client's left side. Press your client's head all the way to her right side until her right ear is resting on her shoulder. Comb and press the wet hair flat against the left side of your client's face and neck so that it sticks to the skin. Cut the surface hair to the same length as the cut hair underneath.

Make another part (approximately 2" from the last part) around your client's head. Clip the rest of the hair back up into the four sections.

Stand on your client's right side. Push your client's head to her left until her left ear is resting on her shoulder. Using the cut hair underneath as a guide for length, cut the surface hair to the same length on your client's right.

Stand in back of your client. Press her head forward until her chin is resting on her collar bone. Using the cut hair underneath as a guide for length, cut the surface hair to the same length in back.

Stand on your client's left side. Push your client's head to her right until her right ear is resting on her shoulder. Using the cut hair length beneath as a guide for length, cut the surface hair to the same length on your client's left.

Repeat taking down 2" partings...

with bent neck, cut your client's right side...

back ...

and left side.

Keep taking down 2" partings...

and cut the right-side...

back...

and leftside of
your client's hair

When all of the hair has been cut, be sure the
hair on both sides is even by standing in front
and cutting any longer hairs.

The entire head of hair should be cut.

Now check the haircut for eveness and possible stray or missed hairs. Roll the head slowly from your client's right, forward and to her left constantly combing the hair flat against her head and neck with the **wide tooth end** of the comb. Cut off any long or uneven hairs.

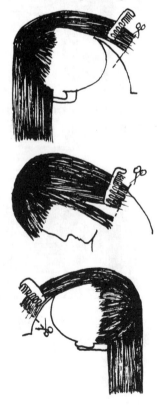

Now repeat the last step rolling your client's head from her left, forward and to her right combing the hair with the **fine tooth end** of the comb. Cut any stray hairs you might have missed.

The 'undercut' is now complete and the hair ready to be styled.

8

CUT 3

THE "BEVELED" CUT

The 'beveled' cut is a slightly layered haircut. Layers are a result of the hair being elevated while being cut. Since layered ends have less weight it creates a softer and fuller look.

Follow the directions for: The Shop Set-up, The Tools, To Start, Handywork and Bangs.

Have your client part her hair where she desires. If no part is wanted, part her hair down the middle to create symmetry.

Using a "T" parting, divide your client's hair into four equal sections. This is done by drawing one part from ear to ear and the second part from center forehead to center nape.

The two parts should cross at the crown.

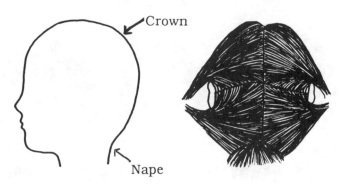

Clip each of these four sections up and out of the way.

Now make a part (approximately one-third inch from the hairline) around the entire head. Clip the rest of the hair back up into the four sections. This will leave a fringe of hair around the perimeter or outline of your client's head.

Comb the fringe hair straight down using the

wide tooth end of the comb.

Look at the following pictures and **choose one that most closely defines the outline of your client's desired haircut.** (Outline 5 has been selected in the pictures throughout this chapter.)

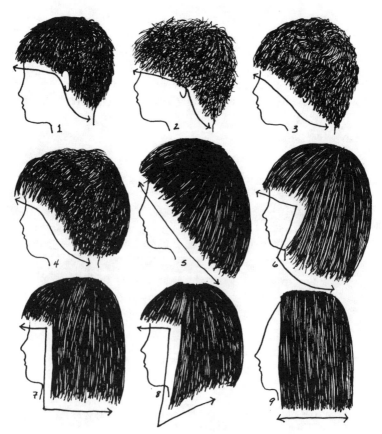

Stand on your client's right. Begin by cutting the fringe hair on your client's right side to the lengths needed to create the chosen outline.

When **cutting hair over the ears**, take care not to nip them. Press the ear flat against your client's head with your less dexterous hand while cutting.

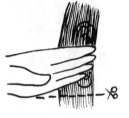

If you are **cutting hair around the ears**, press each ear forward with your less dexterous hand while cutting the hair.

After cutting the fringe on your client's right side to the necessary lengths to create the chosen outline, do the same to the back...

left side...

and front of your client's head.

The fringe creating an outline is now finished. It will serve as a guide for length throughout this cut.

Make another part (approximately 1" from the last part) around the entire head. Clip the rest of the hair back up into the four sections.

Study the following pictures to help decide how much layering your client desires for her hairstyle. **This will determine at what angle**

or elevation the hair should be held while being cut.

Stand on your client's right side. Her head should be held erect and facing forward. Take a small (approximately 2" wide) section of hair between the index and middle fingers of your less dexterous hand. Hold the section of hair tautly at the angle or elevation chosen.

Remember the higher the hair is elevated, the more layering will result.

Now slide your fingers down the hairshaft until the underneath hair falls from your fingers. (The underneath hair does not need to be cut, because it has already been cut).

Stop sliding at this point. You should be able to see the shorter cut hair beneath the surface hair. Holding the hair at the chosen elevation, use your fingers as a straight edge. Cut the surface hairs to the same length and

contour as the hair
beneath.

Repeat the last step moving slowly to your
client's left until the entire parting has been
cut around her head.

Make another part (approximately 2" from the last part) around the entire head. Clip the rest of the hair back up into the four sections.

Stand and begin on your client's right side. Take a (about 2" wide) section of hair between the index and middle fingers of your less dexterous hand. Elevate them to the same chosen angle. Slide the fingers down the hair shafts until the underneath hair begins to fall from your fingers. Stop sliding at this point. Cut the surface hair to the same length as the hair beneath using your fingers as a straight edge.

Repeat the last step moving slowly toward your client's back ...

and left side until the entire parting around

her head has been cut at the chosen angle.

Repeat the last three steps: 1)Take down 2" partings. 2) Elevate a 2" wide section of hair to the chosen elevation, slide your fingers down the hair until the underneath hairs fall, stop sliding and cut. 3) Move slowly to your client's left, until all of the hair has been cut.

Comb the entire head of hair straight down using the **wide tooth end** of the comb. Cut any stray hairs. Now do the same procedure using the **fine tooth end** of the comb.

To check this haircut, hold a vertical section of hair (about 2" wide) between the index and middle fingers of your less dexterous hand. The ends should form a straight vertical line as shown in the following pictures. Cut any stray hairs that stick out from this section.

Now the 'beveled' cut is finished and the hair is ready to be styled.

9

CUT 4

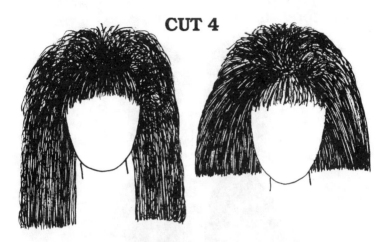

THE "LONG LAYERED" CUT

This cut creates many layers on top, while leaving the weight and length at the bottom which gives height and fullness to long hair.

Follow the directions for: The Shop Set-up, The Tools, To Start, Handywork and Bangs.

Have your client part her own hair where she desires. If no part is wanted, part her hair down the middle to create symmetry.

Using a "T" part, divide the hair into four equal sections. This is done by drawing one part from ear to ear and the other part from center forehead to center nape.

The two parts should cross at the crown.

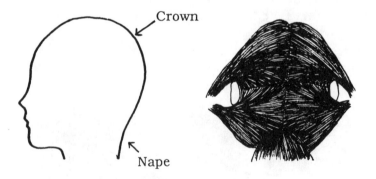

Clip each of these sections up and out of the way.

Now make a part (approximately one-third inch from the hairline) around the entire head. Clip the rest of the hair back up into the four sections. This will leave a fringe of hair around the perimeter of your client's head.

Comb the fringe hair straight down using the wide tooth end of the comb.

Look at the following pictures and **choose one that most closely defines the outline of your client's desired haircut.** (Outline 7 was used in the pictures throughout this chapter.)

Stand on your client's right. Using your 'handywork', cut the fringe hair on her right side to the lengths needed for the chosen outline.

When **cutting hair over the ears**, take care not to nip them. Press the ear flat against your client's face with your less dexterous hand while cutting the hair.

When **cutting hair around the ears**, press each ear forward with your less dexterous hand while cutting the hair.

After cutting the fringe hair on your client's right side to the necessary lengths to create the chosen outline, do the same to the back..

and left side.

The fringe hairs should all be cut to the necessary lengths to create the outline of your haircut. This fringe will serve as a guide for length throughout the rest of this cut.

Make another part (approximately 1" from the last part) around the entire head. Clip the rest of the hair back up into the four sections.

Comb this new parting of hair straight down over the cut fringe using the wide tooth end of the comb.

Stand and begin on your client's right. You should be able to see the cut fringe length beneath the new parting. If not, take down a little less hair so that you can see the cut lengths through the new parting. Using your handywork, cut the surface hairs to the same length as the underneath hair. Work from your client's right, slowly moving toward the back and ending on her left.

This parting should now have been cut around the entire head.

Make another part (approximately 2" from the last part) around your client's head. Clip the rest of the hair back up into the four sections.

Comb this new parting of hair straight down over the already cut hair with the wide tooth end of the comb.

Stand and begin on your client's right. Cut the surface hair to the same length as the hair beneath. Slowly work toward the back and end on her left.

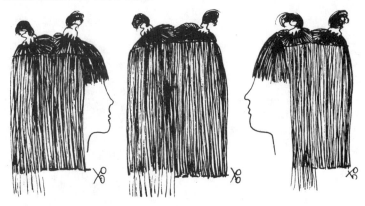

After this parting has been cut repeat the same procedure: 1) Take down 2" partings. 2) Cut the surface hair to the same length as the underneath cut hair (starting on her right, moving toward the back, and ending on her left) until all of the hair has been cut.

Crown

Use the crown as a pivot point by combing your client's hair directly down from the crown as shown in the following picture.

Hold a few strands of hair from your client's crown straight up. Ask her to show you with her fingers exactly how short she wants the layers to be on top.

Measure the strands of hair from your client's scalp to her fingers with the measurements on the comb.

Cut the hair just above her fingers. This will determine the length at which the rest of the layers will be cut.

Hold the cut crown strands up with your less dexterous hand while holding some nape hairs straight up with your most dexterous hand as shown in the following picture.

Draw an imaginary line between the two ends being held up.

(In the beginner's book, "How to Simply Cut Hair", the client tips her head upsidedown while the layers are being cut for a similar effect.)

Your fingers will be held at the same angle as the imaginary line while cutting the hair into layers. The layers will be cut just above your fingers following the imaginary line.

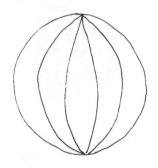

Picture your client's head as a peeled orange with all of the sections exposed.

(Work each vertical orange section from the crown to the nape.)

Stand behind your client and begin on her left. Start with the 'orange' section furthest to your client's left.

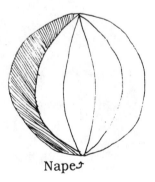

Nape↗

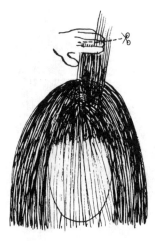

Hold the cut strands at the crown in your less dexterous hand. Position your fingers at the same angle as your imaginary line. Cut the hair just above your fingers following the imaginary line.

Moving down to the next 'orange' section take a few of the just cut strands with some (about 2") uncut hair. Again position your fingers at the same angle as your imaginary line and cut the hair just above them.

Move further down the orange section taking a few just cut strands with some (approximately 2") uncut hair. Again position your fingers at the same angle as your imaginary line and cut the hair above them.

Move (right) to the next orange section.

Beginning at the crown, and moving toward the nape, cut this orange section the same way you did the last one. Cut the hair on the imaginary line just above your fingers.

Repeat the last two steps: 1) Move one orange section at a time to your client's right. 2) Cut each section on the imaginary line working from the crown to the nape.

Do the same procedure in the front by holding a few cut crown strands straight up while holding some cut bang hairs straight up. Draw an imaginary line between the two ends. Cut all of the hairs in between on that imaginary line.

Have your client repart her hair where she desires. If no part is wanted, part her hair down the middle.

Comb the hair straight down using the wide tooth end of the comb. Cut any uneven hairs along the bottom.

Now comb your client's hair straight down using the fine tooth end of the comb. Cut any stray hairs along the bottom.

Now you have completed the "long layered" cut, and the hair is ready to be styled.

10

CUT 5

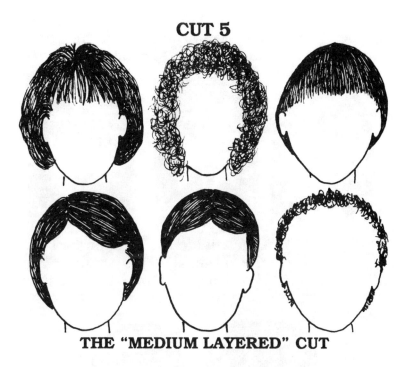

THE "MEDIUM LAYERED" CUT

This cut is for a girl's shorter hairstyle or a boy's long to medium length hairstyle. All the hairs are cut to about the same length.

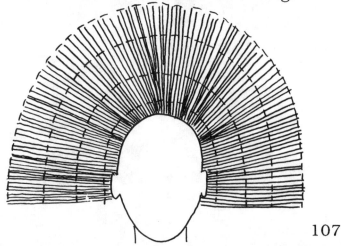

Follow the directions for: The Shop Set-up, The Tools, To Start, Handywork and Bangs.

Have your client part her hair where she desires. If no part is wanted, part her hair down the middle to create symmetry.

Using a "T" part, divide your client's hair into four equal sections. This is done by drawing one part from ear to ear, and the other part from center forehead to the center nape.

The two parts should cross at the crown.

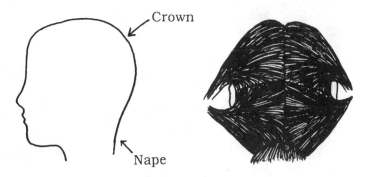

Clip each of the four sections up and out of the way.

Now make a part (approximately one-third inch from the hairline) around the entire head. Clip the rest of the hair back up into the four sections. This will leave a fringe around the perimeter of your client's head.

Comb the fringe hairs straight down using the wide tooth end.

Look at the following pictures and **choose one that most closely defines the outline of your client's desired hairstyle**. (Outline 5 has been selected in the pictures throughout this chapter.)

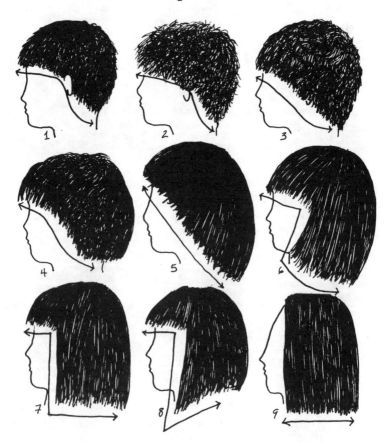

Stand and begin on your client's right. Cut the fringe hair on her right to the lengths necessary for the chosen outline.

When **cutting hair over the ears**, take care not to nip them. Press the ear flat against your client's head with your less dexterous hand while cutting.

If you are **cutting hair around the ears**, press each ear forward with your less dexterous hand while cutting.

After the fringe on the right side has been cut to the lengths needed to create the outline, do the same to the back..

to the left..

and to the front.

Now that the outline is complete, it will serve as a guide for length throughout the cut.

Make another part (approximately 1" from the last part) around the entire head. Clip the rest of the hair back up into the four sections.

Comb this hair straight down over the cut fringe hair using the wide tooth end of the comb.

Stand and begin on your client's right. You should be able to see the cut fringe lengths beneath the new parting of hair. If not, take down a little less hair in the parting so that you can see the cut lengths through the new parting.

Using your 'handywork', cut the new parting of hair to the identical length as the fringe beneath. Work from your client's right moving slowly to her left until the complete parting has been cut.

Make another part (approximately 2" from

the last part) around your client's head. Clip the rest of the hair back up into the four sections.

Comb this new parting straight down over the cut hair using the wide tooth end of the comb.

Using the cut lengths below as a guide for length, cut the new parting to the same length as the hair beneath. Once again work from your client's right, moving slowly to her left until this complete parting has been cut.

Repeat the last three steps: 1) Take down 2" partings. 2) Comb the hair straight down over the cut hair. 3) Cut the hair on your client's right, back and left side, to the same lengths as the hair beneath.

Now the outline has been completed.

Hold a few strands of hair at your client's crown straight up. Ask her to show you with her fingers how short she wants the layers to be.

Measure the strands of hair from your client's scalp to her fingers with the measurements on the comb.

Cut these crown strands just above her fingers. **This will determine the length at which the rest of the layers will be cut.**

Picture your client's head as a peeled orange with all the sections exposed.

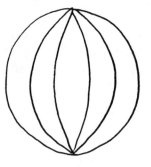

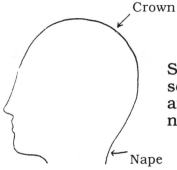

Crown

Nape

Start each 'orange' section at the crown and work down to the nape.

Stand in back of your client. Grasp the crown hairs of the back orange section.

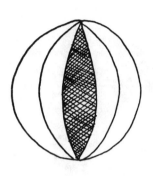

Hold them between the index and middle fingers of your less dexterous hand. The fingers should be positioned vertically (contoured to your client's head shape) at the determined layer length. Cut just above your fingers allowing them to be your cutting guide.

Move down the orange section, cutting the hair to the 'layer length' just above your vertically positioned fingers.

Move to the next 'orange' section on your client's right.

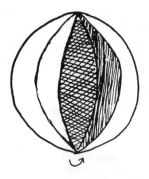

Starting at the crown, take a small amount of cut hair (approximately 1") along with some uncut hair (approximately 1"). The cut hair will serve as a guide for length. Hold this section of hair vertically between the index and middle fingers of your less dexterous hand. Work down the orange section, cutting just above your fingers allowing their contour to be your guide for cutting.

Repeat the last step moving slowly section by section from the back to your client's right.

Repeat the same step moving section by section from the your client's back to her left.

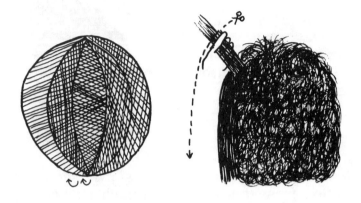

When all of the hair has been layered, comb the hair straight down with both the wide and fine tooth ends of the comb. Cut any stray or uneven hairs along the bottom.

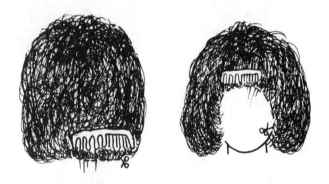

To check the cut, picture your client's head of hair as a cornfield. No matter which way you look down the rows (front, side or diagonal) the rows form straight lines. If the hair is the same length all over, the ends should form straight lines no matter which direction you pull it.

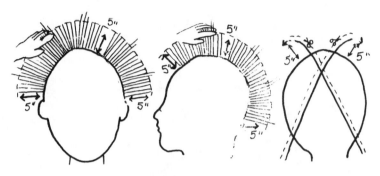

The medium layered haircut is now finished and the hair ready to be styled.

CUT 6

THE "SHORT LAYERED" CUT

The 'short layered' cut is often referred to as the 'shingled' or 'tapered' cut. This tapering can be done just at the nape area, over the ears, or over the entire head. An entire head cut in this method could result in a butch, or crew cut **similar to a razor cut given at a barbershop**.

If a layer length of more than one-half inch is wanted, the **medium layered cut** method should be used. If a shorter length than your finger width (approximately one-half inch) is desired, use the wide tooth end of the comb. If even that leaves too much length you can use the fine tooth end of the comb.

Follow the directions for: The Shop Set-up, The Tools, To Start, Handywork and Bangs.

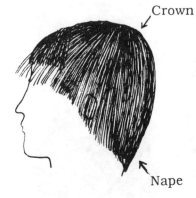

Crown

Nape

Use the crown as a pivot point and comb your client's hair directly down from the crown laying the wet hair flat against his face, neck, and ears so that it sticks to the skin.

Look at the following pictures. **Choose the one that most closely defines your client's desired hairstyle**. This is called the outline.

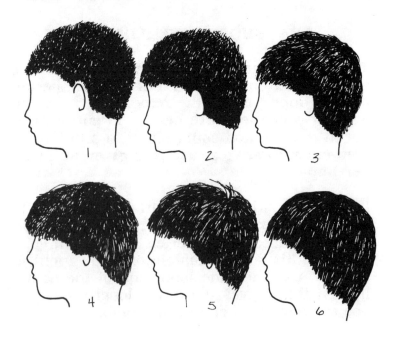

To create this outline, stand in front of your client. Notice that you can see the 'cut bangs' through the longer hairs laying over them.

Cut these long hairs to the same length and contour as the cut bangs beneath. Start on your client's left side, move to the middle and end on his right side.

Now stand in back of your client. Take a section of nape hair (approximately 2") directly in the back of your client's head. Cut the hair to the desired back length. (If you are unsure of the length, have your client help by using his hand to indicate his desired length.)

You will complete this outline by connecting both the front and back lengths. This can be done by cutting both sides of your client's hair. Use the chosen outline as a guide for lengths.

When **cutting the hair over the ears**, take care not to nip them. Press the ear flat against your client's head with your less dexterous hand while cutting.

If you are **cutting hair around the ears**, press each ear forward with your less dexterous hand while cutting.

Stand and begin on your client's right. Use the bang length as a guide for cutting the hair laying beside it. Cut the hair from the front, along your client's right, to the back. The side hair should be cut according to the outline chosen for your individual cut.

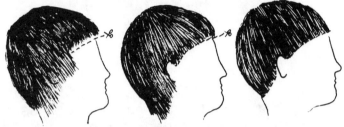

Now you will cut the hair from the back along your client's left side until you meet the bangs. Again, the outline hairs should be cut to the necessary lengths to achieve the outline chosen for your cut.

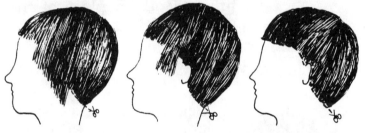

The outline should now be complete.

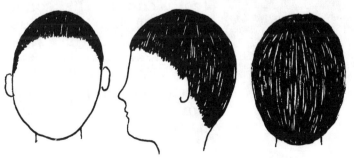

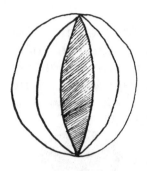

Visualize your client's head as a peeled orange with all the sections exposed. Stand in back of your client and begin at the center section in the back of his head.

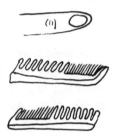

In this book, the wide tooth end of the comb will be used as the determining length at which the client's layers will be cut. If a shorter length is desired, use the fine tooth end of the comb. If a longer length is desired use your finger depth in place of the comb.

Begin at the base of your client's neck with the nape hair. Hold the fine tooth end of the comb with your less dexterous hand, laying the wide tooth end flat against your client's neck. The teeth should be facing upward just below his hairline.

Slowly move the flattened, wide tooth end of the comb up the center orange section in the back of your client's head. The comb will serve as a rake. Cut the hairs as they stick through between the wide teeth of the comb. The cuts will be made just above the comb so that the thickness of the comb is your guide for length. Work from the bottom to the top of the center 'orange' section in the back of your client's head until it is completed.

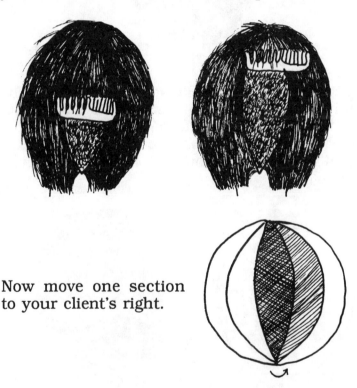

Now move one section to your client's right.

Holding the fine tooth end, place the wide tooth end of the comb against your client's neck. The teeth should be facing upward just below the hairline. Move the comb slowly up the orange section, cutting the hairs as they stick out between the teeth.

Keep moving one orange section at a time, to your client's right. Continue to rake and cut the hair starting at the bottom of each section, working your way to the top of your client's head until you've completed the entire right side.

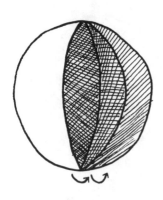

Now do the same procedure, starting at the back and working section by section toward your client's left until the entire left side has been cut.

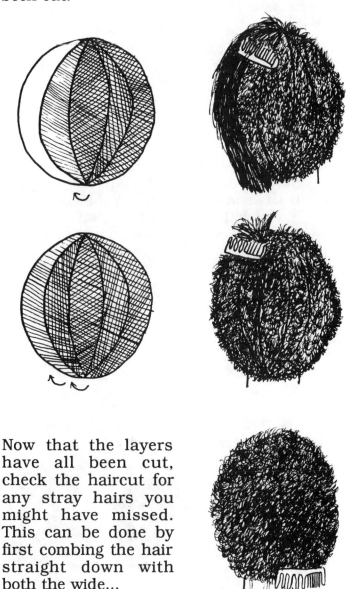

Now that the layers have all been cut, check the haircut for any stray hairs you might have missed. This can be done by first combing the hair straight down with both the wide...

and fine tooth ends of the comb and cutting any long or uneven hairs.

If there are any uneven or choppy lines left behind, rake the hair in an upward direction (from front to back, side to side and diagonally) with the wide tooth end of the comb. Cut any uneven hairs to create a uniform length throughout the cut.

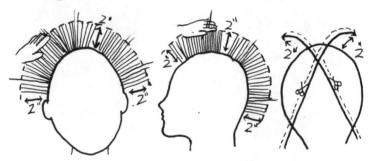

Now the 'short layered' haircut is finished and the hair ready to be styled.

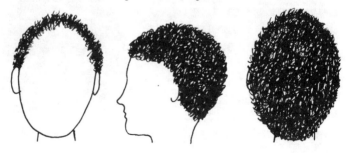

12

ALTERATIONS

Necklines

Use the following pictures to help decide the neckline type your client desires. Begin cutting the neckline hair by starting at one side, working toward the center and ending on the other side. Keep your scissors parallel to the skin to avoid accidentally nipping it.

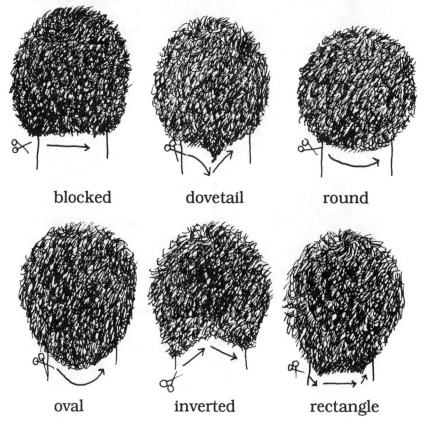

blocked   dovetail   round

oval   inverted   rectangle

Cleaning neck hairs

Lightly scissoring in the neck hairs can give the same appearance as actually shaving the neck hairs. If you don't have an electric razor this method can be used.

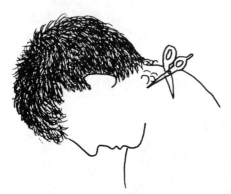

Push your client's head all the way forward. This will stretch the skin and give it tension so that there are no folds or creases of loose skin that can accidentally be nipped.

Hold the scissors in your more dexterous hand, laying them flat against your client's neck. Continually glide the scissors open and closed while sliding them along his neck. Always keep the scissors parallel to the neck to keep the tips of the scissors from nipping the skin. Do this until all unsightly neck hairs are gone.

Sideburns

Use the following pictures to decide on the
length and angle your client wants his sideburns. Keeping the scissors parallel to the
skin, cut the sideburns to the chosen length
and angle. Now use a razor to shave the
sideburn hair below the cut line for a cleaner
look.

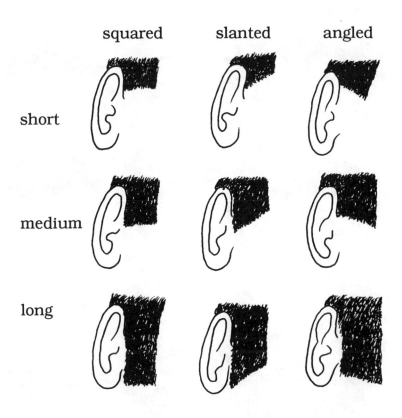

Beards and Moustaches

Use the pictures below to help decide on the style and length of your client's beard and moustache. Always keep the scissors parallel to the skin to avoid nipping the skin. Cut the facial hairs to the desired style and length moving from your client's left toward the middle and ending on his right.

Moustaches

Beards

138

Cowlicks, Widow's peaks and Whirls

Cowlicks

A cluster of hair that sticks up because of the different directions the hair grows from the scalp. They are often located in the front.

Widow's Peaks

A bunch of hair that forms a peak or V shape. They are usually found at the hairline in front or at the nape of the neck.

Whirls

A group of hair that grows in a circular pattern or spinning wheel fashion. They are usually found in the crown area.

Cowlicks, widow's peaks and whirls can be treated by leaving length which adds weight to these problem hairs that stick up, so that they lay down.

Breaking up the "Chop lines"

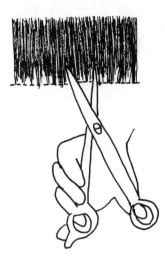

Chop lines are unnatural looking cut marks left by scissors in the hair. They appear most often when cutting straight, fine, blond hair. To camouflage these lines, cut shallow, narrow V shapes into the very ends of the hair These V shapes will break up the harsh, straight edge.

Thinning Hair

There are two ways to thin out unwanted weight or bulk in thick hair. The first way is to use thinning shears. Thinning shears look like a pair of scissors with teeth missing on one or both blades.

These shears are held and used like haircutting scissors. The shears should be held at various angles approximately 3" from your client's scalp. The angle at which the thinning shears are held should constantly change. Thinning should be confined to the bulky areas only and used sparingly so as to avoid creating holes.

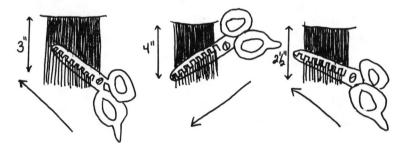

A second way to thin hair (using regular scissors), is to vertically cut deep, narrow V shapes into your client's hair. This can thin out the hair giving it a similar effect as the

3"

thinning shears without having to invest in another tool. Again, thinning should be used in only the bulky or thicker areas to avoid creating holes in your cut.

13

POSSIBLE COMBINATIONS

Combinations is the most exciting and innovative chapter because this is where my teaching ends and your creativity takes over. The only limitation to the millions of hairstyles you can create is your own mind. All of the following hairstyles and more can be done by simply combining two or more of the six basic haircuts and giving them a twist. Even the same haircut can look different by just parting the hair on either side or down the middle, combing it forward or pulling it back off the face. Hair can be sculpted, blowdryed, gelled or left natural.

Each of the illustrated combinations give a front, side and back view of the hairstyle. The combinations are broken down into four categories: outline (page 61), bangs (chapter 5), haircut(s) that are combined (each are separate chapters 6-11) and alterations (chapter12).

Combinations should be attempted **only** after you feel comfortable with each of the six basic haircuts. I hope this chapter encourages curiosity and inspires creativity within you. By simply combining the knowledge found in this book with your own creativity, you can cut just about any hairstyle imaginable.

Outline: 9 **Bangs:** none **Cuts:** cut 1

Outline: 4 **Bangs:** Medium **Cuts:** cut 1

Outline: 5 **Bangs:** none **Cuts:** cut 2

144

Outline: 5   **Bangs:** Medium   **Cuts:** cut 2

Outline: 8   **Bangs:** none   **Cuts:** cut 2

Outline: 8   **Bangs:** heavy   **Cuts:** cut 2

Outline:7 **Bangs:** medium **Cuts:** cut 2

Outline: 4 **Bangs:** heavy **Cuts:** cut 1

Outline: 1 **Bangs:** heavy **Cuts:** cut 5
Alterations: round neckline, short square sideburns

146

Outline: 8 **Bangs:** medium **Cuts:** cut 2

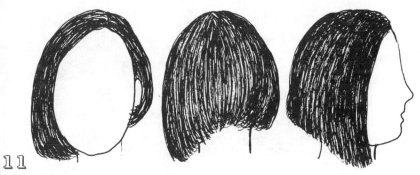

Outline: 8-right 5-left **Bangs:** none **Cuts:** cut 2

Outline: 8-right 5-left **Bangs:** none **Cuts:** cut 1

13

Outline: 9   **Bangs:** none   **Cuts:** cut 1

14

Outline: 7   **Bangs:** light   **Cuts:** cut 1

15

Outline: 7   **Bangs:** medium   **Cuts:** cut 2
(cats-eye shape)

16

Outline:7   **Bangs:** medium   **Cuts:** cut 3-front and sides
cut 2-back

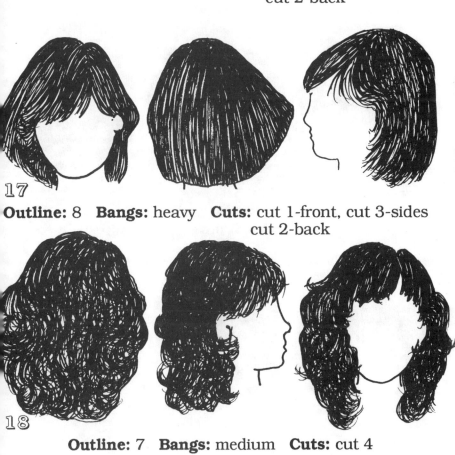

17

Outline: 8   **Bangs:** heavy   **Cuts:** cut 1-front, cut 3-sides
cut 2-back

18

Outline: 7   **Bangs:** medium   **Cuts:** cut 4

149

19

Outline: 4   **Bangs:** heavy   **Cuts:** cut 3 (slightly beveled)

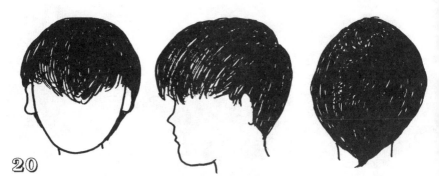

20

Outline: 1   **Bangs:** heavy   **Cuts:** cut 5
Alterations: dovetail neckline

21

Outline: 7   **Bangs:** heavy   **Cuts:** cut 3

150

Outline: 7 **Bangs:** heavy **Cuts:** cut 4

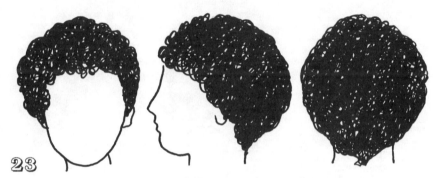

Outline: 2 **Bangs:** heavy **Cuts:** cut 5
Alteratins: dovetail neckline, short slanted sideburns

Outline: 7 **Bangs:** medium **Cuts:** cut 3

25

Outline: 2-lower nape   **Bangs:** none   **Cuts:** cut 6-nape,
Outline 8 rest   cut 5-sides
                                                      cut 2-(rest)

26

Outline: 5-right 7-left **Bangs:** none **Cuts:** cut 3
Alterations: dovetail neckline   (slightly beveled)

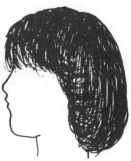

27

Outline: 7   **Bangs:** light   **Cuts:** cut 2-back, cut 3-sides

Outline: 2-lower Nape   **Bangs:** med.   **Cuts:** 5-front and sides, cut 6 back, cut 3 rest   **Alts:** dovetail neckline

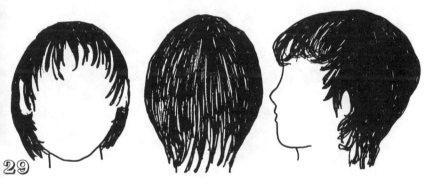

Outline: 7   **Bangs:** medium   **Cuts:** cut 5
Alterations: cut "V" shapes into ends of hair

Outline: 3   **Bangs:** medium   **Cuts:** cut 5
Alts: square neckline,"V"shapes cut into hair ends

153

Outline: 2 **Bangs:** heavy **Cuts:** cut 5
Alterations: square neckline, medium square sideburns

Outline: 1 **Bangs:** medium **Cuts:** cut 5
Alterations: square neckline, medium angled sideburns

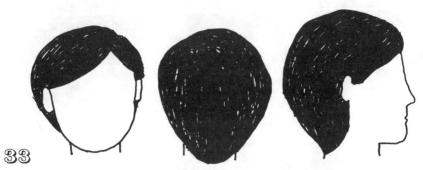

Outline: 1 **Bangs:** medium **Cuts:** cut 5
Alterations: oval neckline, medium square sideburns

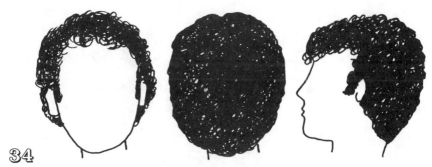

Outline: 1 **Bangs:** medium **Cuts:** cut5
Alterations: round neckline, long square sideburns

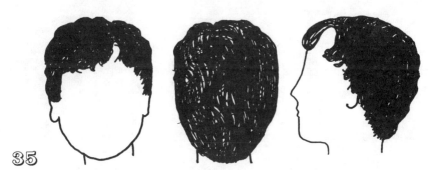

Outline: 2 **Bangs:** heavy **Cuts:** cut 5
Alterations: oval neckline, short slanted sideburns

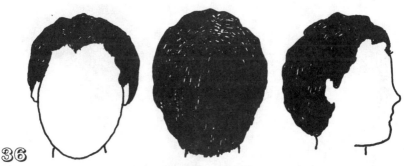

Outline: 1 **Bangs:** medium **Cuts:** cut 5
Alterations: round neckline, medium square sideburns

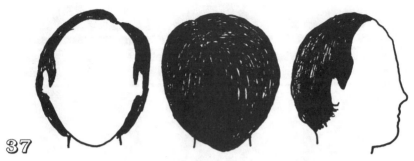

Outline: 3 **Bangs:** none **Cuts:** cut 5
Alterations: oval neckline, long slanted sideburns

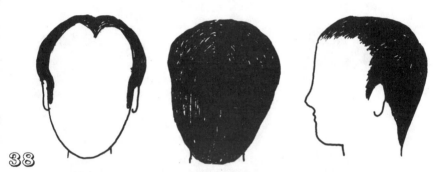

Outline: 1 **Bangs:** medium **Cuts:** cut 5
Alterations: round neckline, long slanted sideburns

Outline: 1 **Bangs:** medium **Cuts:** cut 5
Alterations: square neckline, no sideburns

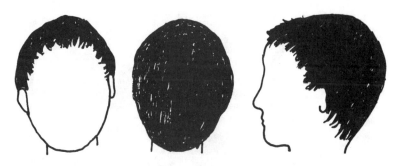

Outline: 2 **Bangs:** medium **Cuts:** cut 5
Alterations: round neckline, short slanted sideburns,
"V" shapes cut into ends of hair

Outline: 1 **Bangs:** medium **Cuts:** cut 6
Alterations: square neckline, medium slanted sideburns, leave length at corners to create square edges

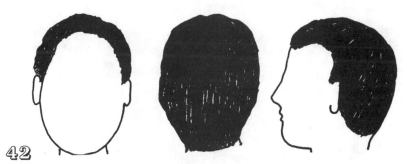

Outline: 1 **Bangs:** medium **Cuts:** cut 6
Alterations: square neckline, short square sideburns

Outline:1 **Bangs:** medium **Cuts:** cut 6
Alterations: oval neckline, short slanted sideburns

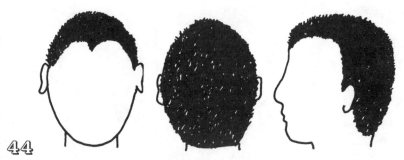

Outline: 1 **Bangs:** medium **Cuts:** cut 6
Alterations: square neckline, medium slanted sideburns

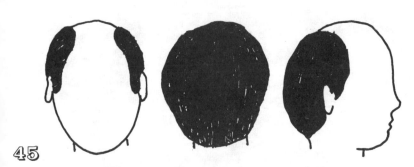

Outline: 1 **Bangs:** none **Cuts:** cut 5
Alterations: square neckline, medium slanted sideburns

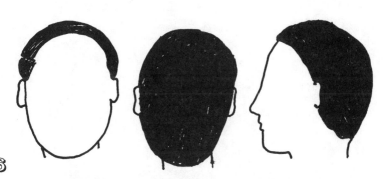

46

Outline: 1   **Bangs:** none   **Cuts:** cut 5
Alterations: round neckline, no sideburns

14

STYLING TIPS

BLOW DRYING

Towel dry as much wetness out of the hair as possible, leaving the hair damp.

Have your client bend forward at the waist. Her head should be tipped completely upside down, letting the hair dangle freely.

Blow dry your client's hair in this upside down position until the hair is barely damp.

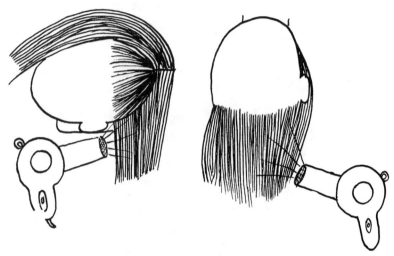

Have your client stand right side up again and part her hair where she desires.

At this point, apply any styling aid such as gel, mousse, lotion, or wave set. This will give body and add extra texture to the hair for a longer holding style. Do this by squeezing a small amount in the palm of your hand. Rub your hands together and distribute it evenly to your client's hair. If your client prefers, the hair may be left natural without any styling aid.

Part your client's hair down the back, dividing it into two sections (one on either side).

Clip these two sections up and out of the way leaving just the bottom third of each section down. (When the underneath hair is dry, it will give the hairstyle more volume, fullness and shape).

Dry the bottom third of the hair, starting at the roots and working toward the ends. Give direction to the hair with a brush or your fingers.

When the bottom third of your client's hair is dry, take the middle third of the hair down from each section. Style it the same way.

When the middle third of your client's hair is dry, take the top third of the hair down from both sections. Style it the same way. Now

your style is complete... unless more curl is desired.

Curl Iron

After your client's hair is completely dry a curling iron can be used to enhance the style by adding curl. The curling iron is generally used to curl just the ends, while hot rollers or curlers give curl to the entire hairshaft.

Use the curling iron sparingly. If clamped down on the ends for too long, dryness and damage may result.

Wrap your client's hair around the curling iron, turning it in the direction you want the hair to curl.

For short hair lay your comb flat against the base of your client's scalp just below the hair being curled. This will protect her scalp from accidentally being touched and burned by the hot iron.

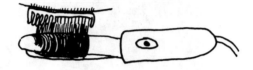

CONCLUSION

Now that you have learned the advanced techniques for the six basic haircuts, isn't haircutting enjoyable?! Taking a boring hairstyle and creating a whole new shape and look can be both exciting and stimulating as well as financially rewarding.

If this book has helped you to discover a natural talent for cutting hair, I would encourage you to consider beauty school. The professional field of cosmetology offers a variety of careers.

TO ORDER: please fill out the order form
and send to:
Punches Productions
P.O. Box 601477
South Lake Tahoe, CA 95702-8
Or Call 1-(800) 833-8778
or 1-(916) 544-7981 inside California

Name

Address

City   state   zip

Phone (   )

Catalog Number	Description		Qty.	unit Price	Total
1001	How to Simply Cut Hair	(Book)		$10.95	
1002	Cutting Children's Hair	(Book)		8.95	
1003	Simply Perm Hair	(Book)		6.95	
1004	Simply Highlight Hair	(Book)		6.95	
1005	How to Simply Cut Hair Better (*Advanced Haircutting*)	(Book)		12.95	
2001	How to Simply Cut Hair	(Video)		29.95	
2002	Cutting Children's Hair	(Video)		29.95	
2003	Simply Perm Hair	(Video)		19.95	
2004	Simply Highlight Hair	(Video)		19.95	
3001	The Basic Haircutting Kit			29.95	
4001	Practice Doll Head			24.95	
	Calif. residents add 7% sales tax				
	Shipping charges add **$1.00** per item				
	Total Cost				

All checks payable to **Punches Productions**. Allow up
to 6 weeks for delivery. Money orders will be shipped
immediately upon receipt. **C.O.D.** charges can be paid
for in cash or money order only.

Satisfaction guaranteed.